COLORADO'S

SCENIC
RAILROADS

Photography by **Bruce Nall**
Text by **Dick Kreck**

Colorado Littlebooks

WESTCLIFFE PUBLISHERS

ENGLEWOOD, COLORADO

ISBN: 1-56579-241-6

PHOTOGRAPHY COPYRIGHT: Bruce Nall, 1997. All rights reserved.
Jan Nall (pages 25, 30, 58), 1997. All rights reserved.

TEXT COPYRIGHT: Dick Kreck, 1997. All rights reserved.

PRODUCTION MANAGER: Harlene Finn, Westcliffe Publishers

EDITOR: Jody Berman, Jody Berman Editorial Services

DESIGN AND PRODUCTION: Rebecca Finkel, F + P Graphic Design

PUBLISHED BY: Westcliffe Publishers, Inc.
2650 South Zuni Street
Englewood, Colorado 80110

Printed in Hong Kong by
Palace Press International

PUBLISHER'S CATALOGING-IN-PUBLICATION

Kreck, Dick.
    Colorado's scenic railroads / photography by Bruce
Nall ; text by Dick Kreck. — 1st ed.
        p. cm. — (Littlebooks)
        Includes bibliographical references.
        ISBN: 1-56579-241-6

    1. Railroads—Colorado. 2. Railroads — Colorado—
History. I. Nall, Bruce. II. Title

TF24.C65K74 1997   385'.09788
                                     QBI97–40825

*For more information about other fine books and calendars from
Westcliffe Publishers, please contact your local bookstore or us by
calling (303) 935-0900, faxing (303) 935-0903, or writing for
our free catalogue.*

FRONT COVER: The Devil's Gate High Bridge on the Georgetown Loop Railroad

BACK COVER: Leaving Rock Tunnel on the Cumbres & Toltec Scenic Railroad

FIRST FRONTISPIECE: Denver & Rio Grande Western Engine 346 operates at the
Colorado Railroad Museum

SECOND FRONTISPIECE: Along the Animas River near Silverton on the Durango &
Silverton Narrow Gauge Railroad

THIRD FRONTISPIECE: Near Cresco on the Cumbres & Toltec Scenic Railroad

OPPOSITE: Leaving Silverton on the Durango & Silverton Narrow Gauge Railroad

Preface

Steam locomotives are fascinating machines. Modern locomotives are powered by hidden diesel engines, but the mechanism of a steam engine operates in full view. Its rods, valves, cranks, and assorted links move in a complex dance accompanied by breaths of steam.

Steam locomotives are also powerful machines. The simple process of converting water to steam to movement occurs on such a large scale that a steam locomotive can pull an amazing number of cars at high speeds.

In the hurried times we live in today, steam train travel is a forced escape from the need to get there now. A steam locomotive cannot be hurried. After being fired, it takes time to heat up, time for steam to build. The complex drive mechanism needs inspection and lubrication.

My interest in steam locomotives and Colorado railroads began in the mid-1970s when I checked out *Narrow Gauge in the Rockies* by Lucius Beebe and Charles Clegg from the library at Kansas State University. I was an electrical engineering student at the time, and the book was definitely not required reading. However, I became fascinated by Colorado in the late 1800s, when mining and narrow-gauge railroads defined much of the development of the Rocky Mountains. I ended up purchasing my own copy of the book and spent many hours studying the photographs and learning about the various routes of train travel.

After graduation and marriage, I vacationed in Colorado, visiting old railroad towns and exploring the remaining narrow-gauge tracks. I moved to

KEEP OFF ROOF

SETTING THE BRAKES
ON A CAR AT THE
COLORADO RAILROAD
MUSEUM IN GOLDEN

Colorado in 1981 and started photographing steam locomotives and trains whenever I could find the time.

To me, witnessing a steam locomotive passing at high speed is like experiencing a rolling earthquake. The ground literally shakes from the power. The sound of smoke and used steam roaring from the stack can be deafening. In contrast, a steam locomotive at rest resembles a sleeping giant quietly breathing wisps of steam. The air pumps thump rhythmically, keeping the air-brake system operational. A generator whines as escaping steam hisses.

The early narrow-gauge steam trains in Colorado were dwarfed by the terrain. The railroads curved and climbed along rivers and struggled up toward mountain passes. Today the preserved routes of trains pulled by steam locomotives pass through rugged and scenic parts of the state. The trains travel at speeds that make the scenery roll by slowly. Although the discomfort of long days of train travel to reach a destination has been dimmed by time, the tourist railroads are long enough to relive the experience but short enough to avoid the pain.

Colorado's tourist railroads offer unique experiences. They offer spectacular views along canyons and rivers, through forests and open meadows. The movement, sounds, and smells transport the rider back to a time when distances were measured in days not hours. I hope the photographs in this book inspire you to visit and ride along.

—*Bruce Nall*

Right: **IN THE SILVER PLUME YARDS ON THE GEORGETOWN LOOP RAILROAD**

Far Right: **UNDER THE DEVIL'S GATE HIGH BRIDGE NEAR GEORGETOWN ON THE GEORGETOWN LOOP RAILROAD**

Colorado Railroads

The names of Colorado's early-day railroads, like the dreams of their builders, were expansive. Faraway places and the promise of great wealth spurred the creation of the Greeley, Salt Lake & Pacific; the Rio Grande Southern; the Pueblo & Southern; the Denver, South Park & Pacific (DSP&P); the Colorado Northern; the Denver & New Orleans, and dozens of other roads. The rush to lay rail was similar to the lure of gold in the Rocky Mountains, where thousands of miners, tantalized by reports of gold strikes, hoped to prove that "Pikes Peak or Bust" was only a slogan. More than 100,000 flocked into the Colorado Territory in 1867, but most only "busted" and returned penniless to their homes in the East.

Many of the pioneer railroad ventures were merely lines drawn on maps, little more than deceptive money-making schemes. Others, like the Boulder, Left Hand & Middle Park, which labored westward from Boulder into the foothills in 1881, actually graded a route for the laying of steel rail but never saw a single piece of rail touch a cross-tie. Some roads that persevered through difficult terrain and withering weather conditions perished when the mines ceased to operate due, in part, to the nationwide economic collapse of 1893. Few of the 35 railroads operating in the young state survived to see the dawn of the twentieth century.

In 1870 Denver was little more than a dusty way station at the western edge of the Great Plains. Visited in summer by miners, trappers, and pioneers, virtually abandoned during punishing winters, the city consisted of

UNION PACIFIC RAILROAD EXCURSION NEAR DEER TRAIL

UNION PACIFIC
RAILROAD ENGINE 8444
OUTSIDE DENVER UNION
STATION

a few buildings and teepees huddled near the confluence of the South Platte River and Cherry Creek and had only 5,000 inhabitants.

When British adventurer Isabella Bird first glimpsed the city, she wrote, "From a considerable height I looked down upon the great 'City of the Plains,' the metropolis of the territories. There the great braggart city lay spread out…upon the brown and treeless plain, which seemed to nourish nothing but wormwood and the Spanish bayonet." Another early visitor described the rough village as "an exceedingly primitive town consisting of numerous tents and numbers of rude and illy constructed cabins, with nearly as many rum shops and low saloons as cabins."

However, in 1870, a miracle occurred for the city's sturdy pioneers. Bypassed by the Union Pacific (UP) in its rush to complete the transcontinental railway across Wyoming in 1869, Denver welcomed the first passenger train of the connecting Denver Pacific Railroad on June 24, 1870. Cheers from a strong turnout of the city's inhabitants and visiting miners rocked the town as the train entered the Mile High City.

The last spike driven to complete the branch from UP's main transcontinental line in Cheyenne, Wyoming, to Denver was made of silver contributed by miners in the Georgetown district. On one side it read, "Georgetown to the Denver Pacific Railway" and on the other, "John Evans, president, June 24, 1870."

In a bizarre twist of history, the silver spike never reached the ceremony in Denver because the high-spirited group charged with delivering it was overcome by thirst at a saloon in Golden. Instead, an ordinary steel spike, wrapped in tinfoil, was substituted. Nevertheless, the Cheyenne-Denver branch was successful. Nine years after the line opened, Denver's population had jumped to 35,000, and by the end of the 1880s 200,000 people lived at the foot of the Rockies. Denver had become a major regional rail center and remains so today.

The first railroads to reach Colorado were the Denver Pacific from the north; the Kansas Pacific, which built east from Denver in July 1870; and the Atchison, Topeka & Santa Fe, which connected southern Colorado to the East, when it reached Pueblo in 1876. Later, they were joined by the Chicago Burlington & Quincy (1881), the Missouri Pacific (1887), and the Chicago & Rock Island (1888), also from the East.

Although these transportation arteries connected Denver and the West to the rest of the country, much of the state's terrain remained unpenetrated in the late nineteenth century. The Rockies, rising abruptly out of the plains to more than 14,000 feet, presented a formidable challenge to even the most dedicated empire builders. Steep canyons and granite peaks, dangerous in the summer and inhospitable in the winter, dared any who would tap the region's rich mineral wealth to enter the high country. Yet by the end of the 1880s, two railroads had conquered the front ranges of the Rockies, and the southern border of Colorado was crossed for the first time.

IN THE SILVER PLUME YARDS ON THE GEORGETOWN LOOP RAILROAD

Left: SILVER PLUME STATION, GEORGETOWN LOOP RAILROAD

Expanding into the Rocky Mountains required finding a less expensive way to build rails along the precipitous hillsides and through the deep, narrow canyons. W.A.H. Loveland, whose Colorado Central Railroad was the first to push into the mountains, discovered the solution. Instead of the standard rail width of four feet, eight and one-half inches, Loveland decided that "narrow-gauge" rails only three feet apart could do the job. Narrower, lighter rails meant track could be laid

without ballast (crushed rock placed under and between the ties to provide stability), and would allow the use of smaller locomotives and cars that could negotiate the tight turns and steep grades. Not to mention that the entire project could be accomplished at nearly one-third the cost of standard gauge.

TAKING ON WATER IN THE SILVER PLUME YARDS ON THE GEORGETOWN LOOP RAILROAD

Left: **CROSSING OVER CLEAR CREEK NEAR SILVER PLUME ON THE GEORGETOWN LOOP RAILROAD**

The Lure of Gold Started It All

One of Colorado's richest mining regions was the Georgetown/Silver Plume district, 51 miles west of Denver on Clear Creek. Between 1860 and 1893, the district's mines produced more than $200 million in gold, silver, copper, and lead. Though these towns and other mining centers were served by various wagon roads, it would take railroads to move large amounts of ore to the smelters downhill in Golden and Denver. Loveland, who helped found the town of Golden, envisioned a monetary bonanza and dreamed of building his Colorado Central through the Rockies and ultimately, he thought, hooking it up with the Union Pacific.

In 1861, Loveland and his partners charted a course through the Rockies. Beginning with a small road company and, later, a railroad line from Golden, Loveland's Colorado Central hauled ore out of the mines around Central City and Black Hawk and returned to the two prosperous towns with supplies and heavy machinery from Denver. Eventually, the line extended up Clear Creek Canyon to Georgetown and Silver Plume.

Like many of the state's early railroads, the Colorado Central struggled financially. By 1872, three years after it was founded, only six miles of grade had been completed to Black Hawk. However, with the aid of a bond issue in Georgetown, the railroad proceeded through Idaho Springs and up the canyon to Georgetown until the first Colorado Central train pulled into the town's depot on August 13, 1877, with 70 passengers onboard. It cost $60,000 a mile to run the line the 34.5 miles between Golden and Georgetown along a route later followed closely by Highway 6 and, still later, Interstate 70.

SUBLETTE, NEW MEXICO,
ON THE CUMBRES &
TOLTEC SCENIC RAILROAD

Next page: TANGLEFOOT
CURVE NEAR CUMBRES
PASS ON THE CUMBRES
& TOLTEC SCENIC
RAILROAD

The most difficult engineering problems were yet to come. Although Georgetown and Silver Plume are only 2.1 miles apart, the steep grade and narrow canyon made switchbacks, the railroad's usual method of scaling heights, impossible. Robert Blickensderfer of the parent Union Pacific Railroad devised a route that looped the track back over itself and incorporated two hairpin turns to climb the 638 feet between the two communities. But the Colorado Central, which later became part of the Colorado & Southern system, had as its goal the rich silver mines of Leadville. Like most pioneer railroads, its ownership was long on vision and short on dollars, in addition to which it had trouble retaining its workers. Laborers frequently signed on with the railroad only to get money and a ride to the mining towns. Others worked a few days, got paid and got drunk, forgetting that they had jobs.

Nevertheless, after a construction delay, the line, including the 95.6-foot-high bridge above Clear Creek that came to be known as "Devil's Gate" on the Georgetown Loop, was completed in January 1884. It immediately became a popular tourist attraction. Advertisements in Denver newspapers proclaimed "no one should miss the Loop trip. The trip is made easily in one day, and at trifling expense." The fare from Denver to Georgetown in 1885 was $3.45, plus another 35 cents to take the dizzying ride over the Loop to Silver Plume.

It was about this time that mining in the region peaked. The railroad struggled on another four miles up the valley to Graymont (today's Bakerville) and there it died, never to reach its Leadville goal. Ironically, there was even

BOXCAR DOOR LATCH

Right: **LEAVING BIG HORN, NEW MEXICO, ON THE CUMBRES & TOLTEC SCENIC RAILROAD**

LOBATO TRESTLE, LOBATO, NEW MEXICO, ON THE CUMBRES & TOLTEC SCENIC RAILROAD

PHANTOM CURVE ON THE
CUMBRES & TOLTEC
SCENIC RAILROAD

discussion of boring a tunnel, known as the Atlantic and Pacific, under Loveland Pass, an idea that didn't become a reality until 100 years later when the Eisenhower Tunnel was constructed.

Even after the ore pinched out, the Georgetown Loop continued to attract tourists. Up to seven trains a day made the trip at the turn of the century, but by 1909 the number of visitors began to decline. The increasing popularity of the automobile and the improvement of mountain roads led to a precipitous slump in ridership and, finally, abandonment of the Loop in 1939 when it was torn down and sold as scrap for $450.

Forty-five years later, thanks to interested citizens and the Colorado Historical Society, the line from Georgetown to Silver Plume —and the historic Loop—were reborn. On August 1, 1984, the new Georgetown Loop accepted its first train loaded with passengers, including Governor Dick Lamm, dignitaries, spectators, and journalists, a train that promptly derailed, putting one car on the ground but injuring no one. Since it reopened, the Loop has averaged 100,000 visitors annually and has brought millions of tourist dollars to the two towns.

CHAMA, NEW MEXICO, DEPOT ON THE CUMBRES & TOLTEC SCENIC RAILROAD

The Survivors Learned to Prosper

The death and rebirth of the Georgetown Loop isn't the only success story among the surviving segments of Colorado's early railroads. The most popular, and probably most photographed, is the Durango & Silverton Narrow Gauge, which wends its way through the rugged San Juan Mountains. The 45-mile stretch of narrow-gauge trackage between Durango and Silverton is one of the last remnants of the once far-flung empire of the Denver & Rio Grande Railroad (D&RG). Unlike many of its contemporaries, the Silverton Branch, known originally as the San Juan Extension, continues to thrive decades after its role as an ore hauler ceased and most of the narrow-gauge lines into Durango and other southern Colorado towns and cities were abandoned and pulled up for scrap.

IN THE CHAMA, NEW MEXICO, YARDS ON
THE CUMBRES & TOLTEC SCENIC RAILROAD

BEHIND THE
ROUNDHOUSE, CHAMA,
NEW MEXICO, ON THE
CUMBRES & TOLTEC
SCENIC RAILROAD

The Race Was On in the 1880s

T he 1880s were a boom time for railroads in Colorado. Anxious to get its share of the transportation pie, the Denver & Rio Grande, faced with much larger competitors, including the Union Pacific and the Atchison, Topeka & Santa Fe, hurriedly built its tracks throughout the state. The first line left Denver in 1871 en route to a projected finish in Mexico. Along the way, the D&RG crisscrossed the state with routes to Pueblo, Walsenburg, Buena Vista, Leadville, Alamosa, and Grand Junction. In 1880 alone, the D&RG built 207 miles of narrow-gauge track statewide.

The D&RG's first passenger train steamed into Durango from Denver to much fanfare and local boosterism on July 27, 1881. One early account bragged, "Men, women and children lined Railroad Street for nearly its whole length…. Members of the City Band assembled at the corner of G and Railroad and commenced playing lively airs, and this of course brought out everybody."

Almost immediately, crews began building trackage toward Silverton, whose surrounding silver-laden hills were producing millions of dollars ("We don't have much gold," an early inhabitant crowed, "but we've got silver by the ton," reportedly giving the town its name). By midsummer in 1882, there were 500 men working for $2.25 a day on the Silverton Branch, which had reached Rockwood, a small settlement 18 miles from Durango.

The most difficult and expensive part of the construction was the High Line, the half-mile-long section blasted out of granite with black-powder

ELK PARK ON
THE DURANGO &
SILVERTON NARROW
GAUGE RAILROAD

charges placed by workers dangling from ropes on the cliff's face. This stretch continues to frighten some riders, perched as it is 400 feet above the roaring Animas River. An incautious traveler could easily step off the train and never touch terra firma before landing in the river's azure waters. Portions of the High Line, which many believe offer the most spectacular views on the entire trip, were used in the 1969 film *Butch Cassidy and the Sundance Kid.*

The Silverton Branch is an engineering marvel and worth the two and a half hours it takes to complete a one-way ride. When the line was finished to Silverton, the *Durango Herald* reported, "The entire distance from Rockwood to Silverton … is through a series of canyons and narrow gorges, with mountain walls of solid granite rising abruptly on either side from five hundred to two and three thousand feet in height … and represents probably the grandest scenery on the American Continent." The Silverton Branch cost slightly more than $575,000 to build, but when completed in July 1882 an adventurous passenger could ride from Denver to Silverton for $37.30, with an additional $4 charge for a Pullman coach.

If building track on the rock-hard edge of the Animas Canyon weren't enough, the railroad was constantly bedeviled by heavy winter snows and avalanches. In 1884, for example, snow began falling in the San Juans on February 2 and continued for 20 days. By February 9, three feet had accumulated in Silverton with drifts up to seven feet. More snow followed and the railroad was blocked for 73 days. In 1886, the line was closed for four weeks; in 1891 for 51 days; and in 1905 for 21 days. Snowslides and rockslides periodically blocked trains, and as recently as 1970 a flood destroyed so much track, most of the summer season's trips were canceled.

ALONG THE HIGH LINE IN THE ANIMAS CANYON NEAR ROCKWOOD ON THE DURANGO & SILVERTON NARROW GAUGE RAILROAD

The Beginning of the End for Mountain Railroads

Abandonment of the troublesome Silverton Branch was discussed frequently, especially after many of the revenue-producing mines and smelters around Silverton closed. The railroad petitioned the Interstate Commerce Commission many times to shut down the line. As early as 1953, a vice president of the railroad warned that if revenues continued to decline the Silverton Branch would have to be closed because summertime tourist visits didn't cover the costs of the high-maintenance line. The Denver & Rio Grande Western, as it was formerly called, abandoned narrow-gauge lines throughout the region by the late 1950s, including the one from Alamosa that connected Durango to Denver.

Thwarted in repeated attempts to abandon the Durango-Silverton route, the Rio Grande decided in 1963 that if it couldn't get rid of the Silverton Branch, it would promote it to tourists, since they made up most of the loads carried anyway. And so it became a lifeline for the once-booming Silverton, served simultaneously by four narrow-gauge railroads in its heyday. Colorado rail historian Robert Richardson noted, "When around noon you see the normally quiet main street suddenly busy with a hundred or more walking tourists, you know it's 'train day' and The Silverton, the only narrow-gauge 'name' train in the U.S., has arrived from Durango."

In 1981, the route was sold to a private owner and renamed the Durango & Silverton Narrow Gauge Railroad (D&SNG) and has become

IN THE DURANGO
ROUNDHOUSE ON THE
DURANGO & SILVERTON
NARROW GAUGE
RAILROAD

one of the state's most recognizable tourist attractions. Having survived economic hard times, snowslides, wrecks, and repeated attempts at abandonment, the D&SNG was nearly ruined by fire in February 1989 when flames devoured the railroad's roundhouse in Durango, destroying the machine shop and damaging several locomotives. The roundhouse was rebuilt and reopened in January 1990 after an investment of $2 million.

Approximately 200,000 visitors, including many hikers, annually ride the Durango-Silverton rails behind smoky, coal-burning locomotives, reliving the days when it took a hardy disposition and a steel posterior to reach into the Rockies.

PRIVATE PASSENGER CAR DOOR ON THE DURANGO & SILVERTON NARROW GAUGE RAILROAD

Left: **PASSING THE SILVERTON DEPOT ON THE DURANGO & SILVERTON NARROW GAUGE RAILROAD**

Men Who Matched the Mountains

General William Jackson Palmer is one of the immortal figures in Colorado railroading. It was Palmer more than any other man who facilitated the building of the Denver & Rio Grande Railroad out of Denver in 1871, its final goal 850 miles away at El Paso, Texas. The few citizens occupying Colorado at the time scoffed at the likelihood Palmer's railroad would live more than a few years, even if it got past the state's southern border. If Denver were small, the population was almost nonexistent south to Pueblo, Colorado Springs, and beyond.

Like Loveland before him, Palmer concluded that the three-foot narrow gauge would be less expensive to build into the mountainous terrain between Denver and Salt Lake City. Palmer was a man in a hurry. The railroad built 74 miles of track between Denver and Colorado City in less than 90 days. Though it never reached anywhere close to El Paso, the D&RG grew rapidly, spreading its track to Florence (1872), Cañon City (1874), LaVeta Pass (1877), Alamosa (1878), and Leadville and Salida (1880). By November 1882, the railroad had reached all the way to Grand Junction on Colorado's western slope.

After a series of financial setbacks and internal fighting amongst its shareholders, the D&RG merged with the Rio Grande Western in 1921 and began an expensive process of replacing some of its narrow-gauge routes with larger, stronger, standard-gauge rail, permitting it to carry longer,

A RAINBOW OVER
ROCKWOOD ON THE
DURANGO & SILVERTON
NARROW GAUGE
RAILROAD

heavier loads. This conversion to the wider gauge, along with the decline of mining, would eventually signal the beginning of the end for the little narrow-gauge tracks that crisscrossed the state. At the railroads' height in 1914, there were 5,933 miles of narrow gauge and standard track in the state. By the late 1940s, branch lines began to disappear, and by the 1950s, abandonments were almost a monthly occurrence.

The Ridgway-Ouray line closed in 1952 and the 10-mile Montrose-Cedar Creek line vanished the same year. In 1953, the Rio Grande was given the okay to drop all lines to Gunnison, and by 1955 the salvage was under way. Finally, lack of freight business caused the D&RG to ask the Interstate Commerce Commission for permission to give up the trackage between Alamosa and Durango, once the pride of the railroad's narrow-gauge system. It appeared only a matter of time before every route would be consigned to the scrapper's torch.

ENTERING A MEADOW ON THE DURANGO & SILVERTON NARROW GAUGE RAILROAD

Saving the Rio Grande from Oblivion

Miraculously, two sections of the vast Rio Grande narrow-gauge system survived. After the D&RG finally succeeded in getting governmental approval to abandon the narrow-gauge line between Durango and Alamosa—the famed San Juan Express route from 1937 to 1950—it ran occasional trips through 1966. Then it died. Weary of the mounting debts and declining freight business, the D&RG wanted out of the passenger trade.

By this time, Coloradans and rail enthusiasts elsewhere were realizing the importance of saving at least a portion of the historic routes. The governments of New Mexico and Colorado stepped in, and in 1970, the 64-mile portion of the line from Antonito, Colorado, to Chama, New Mexico, became a tourist line, renamed the Cumbres & Toltec Scenic Railroad (C&TS) after its two noteworthy scenic sites, Cumbres Pass and Toltec Gorge. The Cumbres & Toltec snakes its way across the New Mexico–Colorado border, offering rail fans and tourists alike unprecedented views. Every year, thousands of riders thrill to the scenery along well-known spots like Phantom Curve, Windy Point, and the famed reverse curve at Big Horn. A leisurely one-way trip on the C&TS takes six and a half hours.

ALONG COLORADO HIGHWAY 550 ON THE DURANGO
& SILVERTON NARROW GAUGE RAILROAD

Mining Wallets Instead of Ore

More than a century later the narrow-gauge railroads, built to facilitate extraction of the Rocky Mountains' wealth, work the wallets of tourists instead of the balance sheets of mining companies. But it was ever thus. The railroads brought the beauty of Colorado's mountain vistas within reach of the average citizen. Then, as now, tourism was an important part of the state's economy, and in their earliest days of operation, Colorado's railroads, built to move ore and freight, quickly became tourist attractions.

Among the most famous tourist rides were Colorado Midland's summertime excursion trains—the Wildflower Specials—begun in the 1890s as one-day trips out of Colorado Springs through Manitou, Cascade, and Green Mountain Falls to the flower-studded slopes near Florissant. Passengers would pluck all the wildflowers they could carry and were permitted to search for fossils and mineral specimens as take-home souvenirs.

The outings were enormously popular, some trips requiring three locomotives and all the passenger equipment the railroad could muster. Many trips included the railroad's elegant chair-observation car number 111, on display since 1960 at the Colorado Railroad Museum in Golden.

Photographs from the period show hundreds of men, women, and children posing beside Colorado Midland locomotives, the women in large hats and white dresses, the men in suits and ties, outfits that must have been more fashionable than comfortable on warm summer days. In 1916, the fare

HERMOSA ON THE
DURANGO & SILVERTON
NARROW GAUGE
RAILROAD

for a 115-mile trip was $1. Unfortunately, the trips proved so popular and the tourists so overwhelmed the fragile mountainsides that the state's official flower, the columbine, was nearly wiped out. Only the demise of the Midland's passenger service in 1918 brought an end to the floral carnage.

The Denver & Salt Lake Railroad, founded as the Denver, Northwestern & Pacific Railway (popularly known as "The Moffat Road," after its founder, David H. Moffat), lured riders with posters heralding "Sight-Seeing Excursions to the Snow Banks on the Crest of the Continent," and proclaiming its route to be the "greatest one-day scenic trip in the world." The Denver Dry Goods department store ran a Moonlight Excursion. There were picnic trains, photographic specials, and trains for religious retreats. The Baptists ran trains for orphans. Even today, The Ski Train to Winter Park operates over the same rails.

ENGINE WATER-GLASS WARNING SIGN

In conjunction with the Georgetown Loop trips, an enthusiastic entrepreneur constructed the narrow-gauge Argentine Central line from Silver Plume to Mount McClellan, carrying sightseers to 13,000 feet. The trip zigzagged up the shoulder of the peak and provided riders with spectacular views. Although it cost a hefty $200,000 to construct at the turn of the century, it closed and was sold for scrap only 16 years later.

Numerous day trips carried city dwellers to the glories of the Rockies. In the 1890s, fishermen's specials ran between Denver and Grant on the South Platte River. At the height of their popularity, two or three trains a day were needed to deliver anglers to their favorite fishing holes. The Denver & Rio Grande ran excursions, using coaches, sleepers, and diners, to carry adventurers to Salida where they would change to narrow-gauge cars that transported them past the Sangre de Cristo Mountains to Alamosa and on to Durango. The trip skirted the southern part of Colorado to Antonito, into New Mexico at Chama, then back to Colorado and visits to Ophir, Telluride, Marshall Pass, and back to Salida. For city dwellers from the dry and arid plains of eastern Colorado, it was a trip unparalleled in its scenic delights.

NEAR THE COLORADO HIGHWAY 550 OVERPASS ON THE DURANGO & SILVERTON NARROW GAUGE RAILROAD

One of the most popular tourist lines was the Denver, Boulder & Pacific, more popularly known as the Switzerland Trail. The line ran from Boulder to Ward, climbing 4,100 feet via Boulder Canyon and close to what is the Peak to Peak Highway today. For 20 years

around the turn of the century, the Switzerland Trail was famous for its excursions to Mont Alto Park, located at 8,600 feet near Sunset, Colorado, where passengers would detrain to picnic and dance in a hall constructed for the purpose. There were outings to nearby Glacier Lake, complete with a baggage car stuffed with lunches and kegs of beer. There were trains for the Fourth of July, Memorial Day picnics, conventions, and political and religious groups.

The Manitou & Pikes Peak Railway, a cog line near Colorado Springs, was built strictly as a tourist attraction. Although rumors of gold in the area ignited adventurers' wanderlust in the 1860s, the 14,110-foot Pikes Peak was more looked at than climbed. Some made the assault on foot, more rode on burros, though it wasn't until June 1891 that passengers of the first scheduled train could ride to the summit in comfort. Today, diesel cars carry 80 passengers on a winding 8.9-mile jaunt to the top where altitude and cold winds frequently have travelers eager to head back down.

One of the state's richest mining regions, where $500-million worth of ore was extracted, the Cripple Creek/Victor area is still home to a narrow-gauge railroad. Once hailed as the "World's Greatest Gold Camp," Cripple Creek at its height was served by three railroads. The region's impressive Cripple Creek Short Line was trumpeted as "the trip that bankrupts the English language." Today, the old Midland Terminal depot, now a museum, stands at one end of Bennett Avenue, the western terminus of the two-foot-gauge Cripple Creek & Victor Narrow Gauge Railroad. Tiny locomotives make a three-mile-long trek to Anaconda, where travelers may detrain and picnic with a view of the Sangres.

CROSSING THE ANIMAS RIVER APPROACHING SILVERTON ON THE DURANGO & SILVERTON NARROW GAUGE RAILROAD

Out of the War, Luxury Travel

After World War II, while the narrow-gauge lines were beginning their slide into oblivion, a standard-gauge, transcontinental beauty made its appearance. Colorado once was home to numerous passenger trains with legendary names, trains where travelers were treated royally with first-class accommodations and dining-car service to rival that of any railroad in the nation. The Shavano, the San Juan Express, the Pony Express, the Columbine, the Rocky Mountain Rocket and, later, during the 1930s era of great stream-liners, the Portland Rose, the City of Denver, the City of St. Louis, and the Denver Zephyr carried thousands of travelers into the state.

Finally, it came down to one, the California Zephyr (CZ), a symphony in stainless steel running between Chicago and San Francisco and operated by the Chicago Burlington & Quincy, the Denver & Rio Grande, and the Western Pacific railroads. It made its debut in 1949 and continued to provide first-class travel until it was discontinued in 1970. The train many called one of the finest ever to be operated in the United States cost $6 million to construct, and included the industry's first domes designed to allow passengers to view the grandeur of the Rockies. In the 1977 book *Portrait of a Silver Lady,* Bruce MacGregor and Ted Benson wrote that the California Zephyr was seen as "mirrors of metal, a visible machine even from the horizon. Its curves were sensuous, even sexual. It arrested speed in its own form."

Until the decline of rail travel in the 1950s, the CZ was the ultimate in luxury. Even after its transcontinental trek was discontinued, the train

continued to operate with top-notch food and service as the Rio Grande Zephyr between Denver and Salt Lake City until 1983. In 1997, it endures under the flag of Amtrak, once again running daily between Chicago and Oakland and giving riders splendid views as it passes through Gore, Ruby, and Glenwood canyons.

As Colorado prepares to enter the twenty-first century, the vanished little engines' larger, more powerful brothers—the massive locomotives of the Union Pacific's vintage steamers 844 and 3985, built in the 1940s to bolster the war effort—make frequent trips into the state for special excursions. Among them is *The Denver Post*'s journey every July to Cheyenne Frontier Days, a tradition that began in 1908 and ran annually until 1970, then was revived for the newspaper's centennial in 1992. It continues to operate behind UP steam, annually carrying a thousand travelers northward to the "Daddy of 'em All" rodeo in Wyoming.

Of the 50 or so railroads spawned in Colorado between 1870 and the middle of the twentieth century, none exists today. Even the ubiquitous Denver & Rio Grande, which survived floods, wrecks, mergers, consolidations, and reorganizations through various reincarnations, was swallowed up by the Union Pacific in 1996.

Some Works of Man Remain

The story of railroading in Colorado is an epic adventure. "In a span of four generations, man brought greater change to those mountains than had all the ages since the outbursts of nature which formed them. Transportation was an essential element in that change, and rail transportation was the most significant part of the picture," wrote Frederick Kramer in his book *Twilight on the Narrow Gauge,* which documented the quick decline and ultimate disappearance of the narrow-gauge lines in Colorado. The railroad builders left behind some of the state's most monumental works. There is the 6.2-mile-long Moffat Tunnel, constructed to avoid a treacherous and often snow-clogged trip over Rollins Pass east of Winter Park. The Moffat Tunnel took four years and $15.6 million to build (the original estimate was $6 million) and cost the lives of 19 workers. The tunnel was the brainstorm of David H. Moffat, but it was the handiwork of surveyor H. A. Sumner that enabled the Denver & Salt Lake to hole through the mountain and cut 175 miles off the route through the Rockies. Plans for the tunnel were discussed as early as 1904, but construction didn't begin until 1923. The opening ceremonies in 1927 were attended by 2,500 passengers on four special trains.

Ironically, with later mergers and acquisitions, the biggest benefactor of the tunnel was to be the Denver & Rio Grande, from which Moffat had been fired as president in 1891. The tunnel continues to be an important link in the state's rail system. Along with the famed Dotsero Cutoff, it remains a

DENVER & RIO
GRANDE WESTERN
CABOOSE 0524 AT
THE COLORADO
RAILROAD MUSEUM
IN GOLDEN

STEAM DOME AND
WHISTLE AT THE
COLORADO RAILROAD
MUSEUM IN GOLDEN

part of the route of the California Zephyr as it crosses Colorado on its travels between Oakland and Chicago.

The narrow-gauge Denver South Park & Pacific, which operated only between 1874 and 1889, ran 151 miles from Denver to Leadville over spectacularly steep grades and was considered an engineering marvel in its day but an ill-advised venture. In addition to its track-laying difficulties on steep grades, the DSP&P took on the ravages of Mother Nature when it constructed the Alpine Tunnel, legendary among rail buffs, at 11,000 feet in the Saguache Range between Buena Vista and Gunnison in 1881. Miners earned $3 a day, and work went on round the clock, even after a single dynamite blast killed 48 workers.

Because the mountain was crumbling and penetrated by underground streams, it required 1.5 million feet of California redwood timbers to keep it from collapsing. Heavy snows were such a problem that after construction was completed, giant timber doors were built on either end of the tunnel that required crews to open them by hand even in the worst weather. Though the tunnel long ago collapsed and was abandoned, the timbers remain in place; the nearby Alpine Tunnel station is a popular tourist destination.

Also constructed during the railroads' halcyon days were the Devil's Gate on the Georgetown Loop, the Rio Grande's hanging bridge at the bottom of the Royal Gorge, and the rail beds carved out of canyons where construction workers were forced to cling to steep mountainsides so often that they came to be nicknamed "squirrels." And there were interurban trolley lines, resort railways, streetcar lines, and trams.

Not Everything Has Disappeared

Though Colorado's early-day railroads have faded into the mists of history, there are still traces of the great rushes to wealth to be seen. Decaying depots and way buildings, steel footings of water towers, rusted rail, and trestles can be found amongst the overgrown weeds and trees by those who know where to look; and some of the grades live on as highways, hiking trails, or Jeep roads.

Much of the memorabilia and flavor from the railroad era lives on at the Colorado Railroad Museum, a small, privately funded repository of the state's glory days in railroading. Founded in 1949 in Alamosa, Colorado, the museum later moved to a 12-acre site just east of Golden. Among the sights there are a large model layout of the Denver HO Model Railroad Club; a bookstore filled with thousands of railroad books, videos, posters, and prints; 50 narrow-gauge locomotives and cars; and the museum's pride and joy, the former Denver & Rio Grande Western steam locomotive number 346, which makes frequent trips around the grounds, its shrill whistle harkening to the days it hauled trains over the narrow gauge.

In 1997, the museum opened the Robert W. Richardson Railroad Library to house photographs, papers, and artifacts, including the early papers of the defunct Rio Grande Southern and the Rio Grande Western, making it a magnet for rail fans and historians.

Lucius Beebe and Charles Clegg, two of the most articulate champions of rail travel in America, wrote in *Narrow Gauge in the Rockies*: "Although

SHORT PASSENGER TRAIN AT THE
COLORADO RAILROAD MUSEUM IN GOLDEN

narrow-gauge passenger operations in the United States were widespread…nowhere did they lend so special a character to the landscape they traversed and the communities they served as in Colorado. Here their identification was complete with every aspect of regional life and regional economy.

Colorado's ample destinies rode the three-foot cars in a special aura of diminutive romance and the impact of their operations were felt everywhere from the Front Range to the Utah line and beyond. In no state of the Union did railroad transport occupy so exalted a position."

SHORT FREIGHT TRAIN AT THE COLORADO
RAILROAD MUSEUM IN GOLDEN

References

Beebe, Lucius, and Charles Clegg. *Narrow Gauge in the Rockies.* Berkeley, Calif.: Howell-North, 1958.

Bollinger, Edward T. *Rails That Climb.* Golden, Colo.: Colorado Railroad Museum, 1979.

Crossen, Forrest. *The Switzerland Trail of America.* Boulder, Colo.: Pruett Publishing, 1962.

Forrest, Kenton, and William C. Jones. *Denver: A Pictorial History,* 3d ed. Golden, Colo.: Colorado Railroad Museum, 1985.

Gale, William F. "Colorado Midland Passenger Service: 1887–1918." *Colorado Rail Annual,* no. 19. Golden, Colo.: Colorado Railroad Museum, 1991.

Kramer, Frederick A. *Twilight on the Narrow Gauge.* New York: Quadrant Press, 1976.

LeMassena, Robert. *Colorado's Mountain Railroads,* vol. 5. Golden, Colo.: Smoking Stack Press, 1966.

LePak, Gregory. *Rails to the Rockies.* Littleton, Colo.: Alpine Publishing, 1976.

MacGregor, Bruce, and Ted Benson. *Portrait of a Silver Lady.* Boulder, Colo.: Pruett Publishing, 1977.

Morgan, Gary. *Rails Around the Loop.* Fort Collins, Colo.: Centennial Publications, 1976.

Noel, Thomas J. *The City and the Saloon: Denver 1858–1916.* Niwot, Colo.: University Press of Colorado, 1996.

Ormes, Robert M. *Railroads and the Rockies.* Denver: Sage Books, 1963.

Osterwald, Doris B. *Beyond the Third Rail.* Lakewood, Colo.: Western Guideways, 1994.

Osterwald, Doris B. *Cinders and Smoke.* Lakewood, Colo.: Western Guideways, 1965.

Richardson, Robert W. "Narrow Gauge News." *Colorado Rail Annual,* no. 21. Golden, Colo.: Colorado Railroad Museum, 1994.

Sibert, Edgar H., and Ted S. McKee. *Railfan's Guide to Colorado.* Boulder, Colo.: Pruett Publishing, 1982.

Smiley, Jerome. *History of Denver.* Denver: Old Americana Publishing, 1901.

Wilkins, Tivis E., *Colorado Railroads: Chronological Development.* Boulder, Colo.: Pruett Publishing, 1974.